•••◉ BULLETPOINTS ◉•••

EARLY HUMANS

Andrew Campbell
Consultant: Steve Parker

Miles Kelly
PUBLISHING

First published in 2005 by Miles Kelly Publishing Ltd
Bardfield Centre, Great Bardfield
Essex, CM7 4SL

Some of this material also appears in the *1000 Facts* series and the *Visual Factfinder* series

2 4 6 8 10 9 7 5 3 1

Editorial Director: Belinda Gallagher

Editorial Assistant: Amanda Askew

Picture researcher: Liberty Newton

Production: Estela Boulton

Scanning and reprographics: Anthony Cambray, Mike Coupe, Ian Paulyn

British Library Cataloguing-in-Publication Data
A catalogue record for this book is available from the British Library

ISBN 1-84236-552-5

Printed in China

www.mileskelly.net
info@mileskelly.net

Contents

Hominid fossils

- **The fossil record** of hominids (human ancestors) is very patchy.

- **Most early hominid fossils** have been discovered in the Great Rift Valley region of East Africa, which stretches through Ethiopia, Kenya and Tanzania.

- **Probably the most important** site for evidence of human ancestors is Olduvai Gorge in northern Tanzania.

▼ *The Laeotoli footprints left by two* Australopithecus afarensis *individuals were proof that early hominids walked on two legs.*

- **Archaeologists** have discovered fossils from more than 50 hominids at the Gorge, including *Australopithecus boisei*, *Homo habilis*, *Homo erectus* and a 17,000-year-old *Homo sapiens*.

- **Complete hominid skeletons** are very rare. Archaeologists usually have to rely on skulls, knee joints or even single teeth.

- **Another type of fossil** remain is a trace fossil, such as tracks and footprints.

- **The most famous hominid** trace fossil is the footprints that were left by two *Australopithecus afarensis* individuals. The prints were made in wet, sandy ground and were then covered in ash from an erupting volcano.

- **This fossil footprints were discovered** in 1978 by the archaeologist Mary Leakey (1913–1996). They are known as the Laeotoli footprints, after the site in Tanzania where she found them.

- **Caves** are second only to rivers and lakes as good sites for fossils, since bodies are less likely to be disturbed there. Most hominid fossils in southern Africa are from caves.

- **Scientists** can tell from hominids' teeth what they ate. Unlike earlier hominids, *Homo erectus* was a meat eater because its teeth are scratched and damaged.

Walking upright

- **Hominidae** is the 'human family' of ourselves and our ancestors and prehistoric relatives. Hominids (humans) differed from apes by walking on two legs, rather than four.

- **Fossils** of hominids' backbones, neck, foot and leg bones demonstrate their evolution from apes that walked on all fours.

- **Hominids'** spines developed an S-shaped curve so that the hips supported the weight of the upper body. Apes' spines have just one curve.

- **The heads of the hominids** evolved to sit on the top of the spine, while apes' heads sit at the front of the spine.

- **Hominids'** feet became long and flat to support the rest of the body when they walked. Apes' feet have curved toes to grasp onto branches for climbing.

- **The leg bones of hominids** became longer and straighter than those of apes, so they could walk greater distances more effortlessly.

- **Walking on two legs** helped hominids cover greater distances in the open grasslands of Africa where they lived.

- **It also allowed them** to see above tall grasses, an advantage when it came to looking for food or keeping a lookout for danger.

- **Upright walking** also freed their arms to do other things, such as carrying babies or food.

> ...FASCINATING FACT...
> The first fossilized footprints of an upright walker
> were discovered in 1978. They belong to
> *Australopithecus afarensis*, which lived 3.8 mya.

Homo habilis

Homo erectus

Homo neanderthalensis

Homo sapiens

▲ *Experts agree that the adoption of upright walking was one of the most important developments in the history of hominids. It freed the arms and hands to carry objects, making the body look bigger to potential predators and keeping it cool in the hot Sun.*

Early hominids

▲ Ardipithecus ramidus. *Scientists gave it its name from the Afar language of Ethiopia – 'ardi' means 'ground' while 'ramid' means 'root' – words that express its position at the base of human history.*

- **One of the earliest-known** hominids (early humans) is *Ardipithecus ramidus,* which lived about 4.5 mya.

- **It would have looked** similar to a chimpanzee in many ways, except for one major difference, *Ardipithecus ramidus* walked on two legs.

- **It lived** in woods and forests, sleeping in trees at night, but foraging on the ground for roots during the day.

- **A full-grown** *Ardipithecus ramidus* male was about 1.3 m tall and weighed about 27 kg.

- **Archaeologists** discovered the teeth, skull and arm bone fossils of *Ardipithecus ramidus* in Ethiopia in 1994.

- **In 2001**, archaeologists in Ethiopia found the remains of an even older hominid, *Ardipithecus ramidus kadabba*, which lived between 5.6 and 5.8 mya.

- **The fossils** of *Ardipithecus ramidus kadabba* are similar to those of *Ardipithecus ramidus,* so it is possible both are very closely related.

- **Some scientists argue,** however, that *Ardipithecus ramidus kadabba* is closer to an ape than a hominid.

- ***Australopithecus anamensis*** is a later hominid than *Ardipithecus ramidus.* Its fossils date to between 4.2 and 3.9 million years old.

- **A fossil** of one of *Australopithecus anamensis'* knee-joints shows that it shifted its weight from one leg to the other when it moved – a sure sign that it walked on two legs.

Sahelanthropus tchadensis

- **In 2002**, a team of French archaeologists announced the discovery of a new species called *Sahelanthropus tchadensis,* which may be a missing link between apes and early hominids.

- **The archaeologists** discovered a near-complete fossil skull of *Sahelanthropus tchadensis*, which has been dated to between 7 and 6 million years old.

- **They also** found the fossils of two pieces of jawbone and three teeth.

- **The French team** found the skull not in East Africa, like all the other early hominids, but in Chad, in central Africa.

- **Finding the skull** in Chad indicates that early hominids ranged well beyond East Africa, where scientists previously believed all early hominids lived.

- **The archaeologists** who discovered the skull nicknamed it Toumaï, meaning 'hope of life' in Goran, an African language.

- **Despite its great age,** *Sahelanthropus tchadensis'* skull suggests that it had a surprisingly human face, which protruded less than apes.

- *Sahelanthropus tchadensis* also had heavy ridges for its eyebrows. Some archaeologists believe that, because of this, it was closer to an ape than a hominid, since female apes have similar heavy ridges.

- **Like later hominids,** *Sahelanthropus tchadensis* had small canine teeth and did not grind its teeth in the same way as apes.

- *Sahelanthropus tchadensis* lived alongside a diverse range of animals. Other fossil finds in the same region include more than 700 types of fish, crocodiles and rodents.

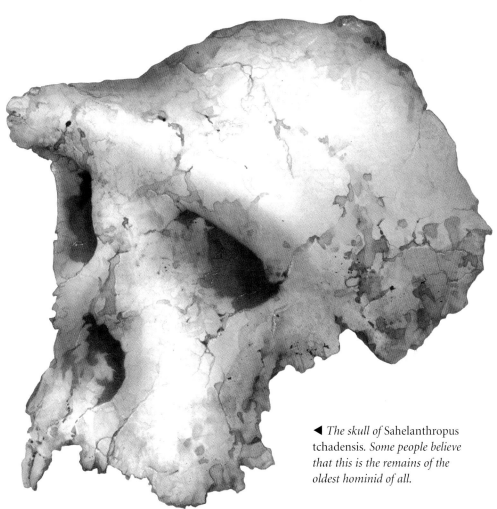

◀ *The skull of* Sahelanthropus tchadensis. *Some people believe that this is the remains of the oldest hominid of all.*

Australopithecus afarensis

- *Australopithecus afarensis* was an early hominid that lived 3.5 mya.

- **Its brain** was the size of a modern chimpanzee's, and it had the short legs and long arms of modern apes.

- *Australopithecus afarensis* only measured between 90 and 120 cm.

- **Like other** australopithecines, it walked on two legs. This was the most efficient way for it to move over grassland in search of food.

- **It had a wider pelvis** and shorter legs than modern humans. This may have made it a more efficient walker than modern humans.

- *Australopithecus afarensis* ate seeds, fruits, nuts and occasionally meat.

- **These hominids** had a brief childhood, reaching adulthood at the age of 11 years old. They lived for a maximum of 50 years.

- **Fossil footprints** of *Australopithecus afarensis* show that their feet were similar to ours, although their big toes may have been more apelike.

- **The first fossils** of *Australopithecus afarensis* to be discovered belonged to a female. They were found by American anthropologists Donald Johanson and Tom Gray in 1974, at Hadar in Ethiopia.

> ...FASCINATING FACT...
> Johanson and Gray named the female 'Lucy' after the Beatles' song 'Lucy in the Sky with Diamonds', which they listened to on the day of their discovery.

▲ Australopithecus afarensis *spent its days on the ground, foraging for food, but at night may have slept in trees.*

Australopithecus africanus

- *Australopithecus africanus*, which means 'the southern ape of Africa', was an early hominid that emerged between 2.8 and 2.3 mya.

- *Australopithecus africanus* was the first australopithecine to be discovered.

- **The Australian-born** scientist Raymond Dart made the discovery of this important fossil in South Africa in 1924.

- **The fossil** Dart identified was found in a quarry near the village of Taung, on the edge of the Kalahari Desert.

- **It was the fossil** of a skull, belonging to a child around 2 or 3 years old. The fossil became known as the Taung child.

- **Many people** didn't believe in Dart's discovery – they thought the find was an ape, not a hominid. But one person did believe it – the archaeologist Robert Broom.

- **In 1947** Broom himself found a skull of an adult *Australopithecus africanus*.

- **The adult skull** became known as 'Mrs Ples' because Broom first thought it belonged to a different species, *Plesianthropus transvaalensis*.

- **By the 1950s** other parts of *Australopithecus africanus*' skeleton had been unearthed, including a pelvis and a femur.

- **They proved** beyond doubt that *Australopithecus africanus* was an upright-walking hominid.

▶ *The Taung child may have looked like this. Marks on the skull, and remains of a large eggshell nearby, suggest a large bird killed the child.*

Paranthropus boisei

- *Paranthropus boisei* was a hominid that lived between one and two mya.

- **It had much bigger** jaws and teeth than modern humans but much smaller bodies. Males grew to about 137 cm tall.

- **Male skulls** were more than twice as big as female skulls because they had large crests of bone on the top, to which powerful chewing muscles were fixed. Females did not have these muscles.

- *Paranthropus boisei* was one of several different hominid groups that developed in East Africa between 2.8 and 2.5 mya in response to climate change.

- **Different hominids** developed to exploit different resources. *Paranthropus boisei* evolved as a specialist eater of very hard, abundant, but low-quality plant foods like roots and tubers.

- **In contrast**, more advanced hominids such as *Homo habilis* and *Homo rudolfensis* evolved to vary their diets and to seek out high-quality foods.

- **Because it was such a successful** plant eater, *Paranthropus boisei* forced other hominids to become omnivores, eating whatever they could find.

- **The first *Paranthropus boisei*** was discovered in Tanzania in 1959 by the archaeologists Louis and Mary Leakey.

- **The Leakeys** named their find after the businessman Charles Boise who had supported their work. Paranthropus means 'near man'.

- **Unlike modern humans**, there were no whites to *Paranthropus boisei's* eyes, so one individual could not tell where another was looking, or what it was feeling.

◀ *These* Paranthropus boisei *hominids were another species of australopithecine ('southern ape'). The males had particularly large jaws and robust skulls.*

Homo habilis

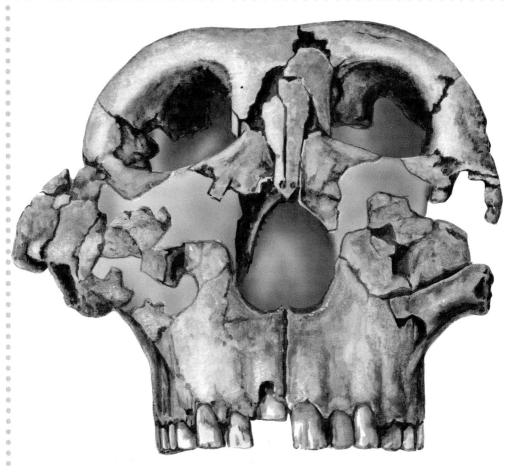

▲ *The first* Homo habilis *skull found by Louis and Mary Leakey in Tanzania.* Homo habilis *had a bigger brain than any previous hominid.*

- *Homo habilis* is one of the earliest-known members of the genus *Homo*, to which we also belong.

- *Homo habilis* lived between 2.4 and 1.6 mya.

- **The archaeologists** Louis and Mary Leakey first discovered its remains at Olduvai Gorge in Tanzania, in 1961.

- **Fossils** of *Homo habilis'* skulls have since been found around Lake Turkana in Kenya, one of the richest sites for hominid fossils in the world.

- **The skulls** show that *Homo habilis* had a flat face with prominent cheekbones, similar to australopithecines, which it would have lived alongside.

- *Homo habilis* was much more ape-like than its successor, *Homo ergaster*. It had fur and lacked any form of language.

- **But it did have** a bigger brain than any australopithecine. It also had more flexible hands and straighter, more sensitive fingers.

- *Homo habilis* means 'handy man' – it could use its hands to gather fruit and crack nuts. It also created the first stone tools.

- **A fully grown** *Homo habilis* male was around 1.5 m tall and weighed about 50 kg.

...FASCINATING FACT...
Homo habilis used stone tools to crack open animal bones so it could eat the nutritious marrow inside.

Homo ergaster

- *Homo ergaster* was the first 'human-looking' early human. It first appeared about 1.9 mya.

- **Adult males** grew to approximately 180 cm tall, with long, slender limbs and a straight spine.

- *Homo ergaster* was the first smooth-skinned hominid, unlike its hairy ancestors. Like us it cooled down by sweating, not panting, which is how earlier hominids cooled themselves.

- **It was also** the first hominid to have a protruding nose – previous hominids merely had nostrils on the surface of their face.

- *Homo ergaster* was generally a scavenger, although it would hunt and kill older or weaker animals.

- **Scientists** know that it ate a lot of meat because one of the skeletons that have been found shows evidence of a bone disease caused by eating too many animal livers.

- **Fossil remains** of *Homo ergaster* were first discovered in 1975. But the most complete skeleton was found in 1984.

- **The skeleton** belonged to a teenage boy named Nariokotome Boy after the site in Lake Turkana, Kenya, where it was found.

- **The structure** of Nariokotome Boy's bones suggest that he was much stronger than modern humans.

- *Homo ergaster* was the first hominid to travel beyond Africa. One place where its remains have been found is Dmanisi, in the Republic of Georgia, near Russia.

▶ Homo ergaster *was different from any previous hominid. It was taller, with a face that was more lightly built and had smaller cheek teeth.*

21

Homo erectus

- *Homo erectus* may be a descendant of *Homo ergaster*.

- **It was** virtually identical to its immediate ancestor, except that it had thicker bones in its skull and a more protruding eyebrow ridge.

- *Homo erectus* and *Homo ergaster* lived alongside each other for 2 million years.

- **But while *Homo ergaster*** became extinct about 600,000 years ago, *Homo erectus* survived until less than 50,000 years ago.

- *Homo erectus* spread beyond Africa and settled in Europe and Asia.

- **In the late 19th century,** Eugène Dubois discovered *Homo erectus* fossils on the Indonesian island of Java. He was a famous Dutch palaeoanthropologist (someone who studies hominid fossils).

- **In the 1930s,** archaeologists discovered more than 40 *Homo erectus* skeletons in China.

- **The archaeologists** also found evidence that *Homo erectus* used fire and practised cannibalism!

- **For a long time**, people called the human to which the Chinese fossils belonged 'Peking Man'. It was much later that palaeoanthropologists realized it was, in fact, *Homo erectus*.

> ...FASCINATING FACT...
> The 'Peking Man' fossils disappeared at the beginning of the World War II and have never been found. They were confiscated by Japanese troops just when they were about to be shipped to the USA.

▲ *Stone hearths in caves that were used by* Homo erectus *prove that it had mastered fire.*
Fire provided warmth, light, protection and the means to cook food.

Homo heidelbergensis

▲ Homo heidelbergensis *was a superb hunter who used stones, wooden spears and even stone blades to capture food.*

- *Homo heidelbergensis* lived between 600,000 and 250,000 years ago in Africa and Europe.

- **It was the first** hominid to settle in the cold territories of northern Europe.

- **Homo heidelbergensis** had a body much like ours, but its head was rather different, with a heavier jaw, a minimal chin, a flat nose and thick eyebrow ridges.

- **The teeth** of *Homo heidelbergensis* were 50 percent longer than ours.

- **They also** had a much thicker covering of enamel, which suggests that this species ate the tough parts of animals' flesh and maybe used its teeth for gripping objects.

- **Towards the end** of its existence, *Homo heidelbergensis* would have lived alongside Neanderthals in the same territories.

- *Homo heidelbergensis* is named after the city of Heidelberg in Germany. It was near there that one of the hominid's jawbones was found in 1907.

- **The greatest find** of *Homo heidelbergensis'* fossils was made in a cave system in the Atapuerca hills of northern Spain, in 1976. Archaeologists discovered the remains of 32 individuals.

- **In the mid 1990s**, archaeologists unearthed *Homo heidelbergensis* bones, tools and animal carcasses in Boxgrove, England. The carcasses had been expertly stripped of all their meat.

> ... **FASCINATING FACT** ...
> Unlike the Neanderthals that came later, there is no
> evidence that *Homo heidelbergensis* buried its dead.

Homo neanderthalensis

- *Homo neanderthalensis* – or Neanderthals – lived between 230,000 and 28,000 years ago across Europe, Russia and parts of the Middle East.

- *Homo neanderthalensis* **means** 'man from the Neander Valley', which is the site in Germany where the first of its fossil remains were found in 1865.

- **Neanderthals** are our extinct cousins rather than our direct ancestors – they are from a different branch of the human family.

- **They were** about 30 percent heavier than modern humans. Their bodies were more sturdy and they had shorter legs.

- **Neanderthals'** shorter, stockier bodies were better suited than modern humans to life in Europe and Russia during the ice ages of the Pleistocene Epoch (1.6 million to 10,000 years ago).

- **Their faces** were also different, with sloping foreheads and heavy brow ridges.

- **They buried** their dead, cooked meat and made various tools and weapons.

- **Neanderthals** made the first ever spears tipped with stone blades.

- **For about 10,000 years** Neanderthals lived alongside modern humans in Europe, before becoming extinct.

> ### FASCINATING FACT
> Many people think that Neanderthals were slow and stupid, but in fact their brains were at least as big as modern human's.

Homo floresiensis

- **In 2004**, Australian palaeoanthropologists discovered an entirely new species of human, *Homo floresiensis,* which lived on the Indonesian island of Flores between 95,000 and 13,000 years ago.

- **In total**, palaeoanthropologists have unearthed the remains of seven individuals.

- **The most complete**, although still partial, skeleton, is that of a female. Study of one of its leg bones shows that it was an upright walker.

- **The discovery** changes scientists' understanding of human evolution – beforehand, it was assumed that *Homo sapiens* had been the sole remaining human species since the disappearance of Neanderthal humans about 30,000 years ago.

- **Palaeoanthropologists** nicknamed *Homo floresiensis* 'hobbit man' because of its tiny size. It was about one metre tall, and had a brain the size of a chimpanzee's.

- **Its small brain size** does not seem to have reflected its intelligence however – *Homo floresiensis* was a skilled toolmaker, producing finely crafted stone tools.

- **Flores**, off the coast of mainland Asia, has been an island for over a million years. Being small represents an adaptation to living on an isolated island, where resources were limited.

- ***Homo floresiensis'*** small size challenges the accepted belief that humans modify their surroundings to suit themselves. It is believed that, on the contrary, this human species evolved into a smaller creature to cope with its island habitat.

▶ *Two* Homo floresiensis *hunters prepare to attack a pygmy elephant. The discovery of this new species of human challenges our ideas of human evolution.*

- **Local inhabitants** of Flores have long told stories of little hairy people called *ebu gogo*, meaning 'grandmother who eats anything'.

- ***Homo floresiensis*** was a hunter. One of the animals it preyed on was the pygmy elephant. Both *Homo floresiensis*, and the pygmy elephants seem to have become extinct after a volcanic eruption about 12,000 years ago.

Homo sapiens

- *Homo sapiens* – meaning 'wise man' – first appeared in Africa around 150,000 years ago. This is the species to which human beings belong.

- **The first** *Homo sapiens* outside Africa appeared in Israel, 90,000 years ago.

- **By 40,000 years ago**, *Homo sapiens* had spread to many parts of the world, including Europe and Borneo.

- **We call the humans** that settled in Europe Cro-Magnons. They dressed in furs and hunted with spears and nets.

- **Cro-Magnons** had a basic language and culture, which included painting images on cave walls.

- **They were** very similar to modern humans, but with marginally bigger jaws and noses and more rounded braincases (the part of the skull that encloses the brain).

- *Homo sapiens* probably arrived in North America about 30,000 years ago.

- **They would have** crossed the Bering land bridge – formed by shrunken sea levels during the then ice age – from present-day Siberia to present-day Alaska.

- **The earliest known** human culture in North America is that of the Clovis people, which is thought to be around 11,500 years old.

> **· · · FASCINATING FACT · · ·**
> Humans living today have evolved only slightly from the earliest *Homo sapiens*. Our full scientific name is *Homo sapiens sapiens*, which means 'the wise wise man'.

▲ *Cave painting, cooking and complicated tool-making are all features of early* Homo sapiens. Homo sapiens *also look different from other human species, having a higher forehead and a more prominent chin.*

Brains and intelligence

- **Primates**, from which hominids descended, had bigger brains in relation to their body size than other mammals.

- **Primates developed** larger brains – and more intelligence – because living in and moving between trees required a high degree of balance, coordination and the skilful use of hands and feet.

- **Once hominids' brains** started getting bigger, so their skulls began to change. Bigger brains led to the development of foreheads.

- *Homo habilis'* **brain** was 50 percent bigger than its australopithecine predecessors. It had a brain capacity of 750 ml.

- **The structure** of its brain was different to that of earlier hominids. It had much bigger frontal lobes – the parts of the brain associated with planning and problem-solving.

- *Homo habilis* put its greater intelligence to use in the quest to find meat, which it scavenged from other animals' kills to supplement its diet.

- **Eating more meat** allowed hominids' brains to get even bigger. Breaking down plant food uses up a huge amount of energy, so the fewer plants hominids ate, the more energy was available for their brains.

- *Homo ergaster* had an even bigger brain, with a capacity of around 1000 ml. It could use this intelligence to read tracks left by animals – a major development in hunting.

- **The brain** of *Homo erectus* became larger during its existence. About 1 mya its brain capacity was 1000 ml; 500,000 years later it was 1300 ml.

- **Our brain capacity** is 1750 ml.

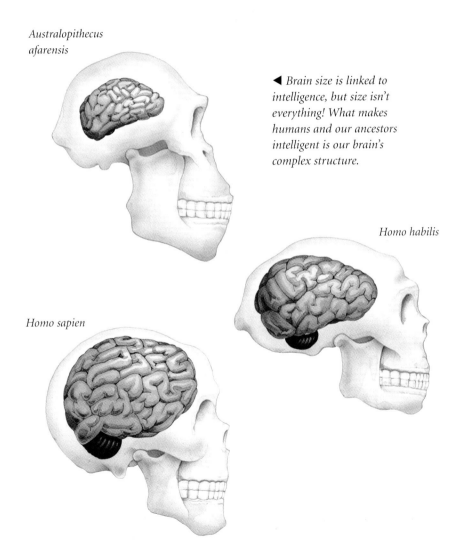

*Australopithecus
afarensis*

◀ *Brain size is linked to
intelligence, but size isn't
everything! What makes
humans and our ancestors
intelligent is our brain's
complex structure.*

Homo habilis

Homo sapien

Language

- **Language** may go back as far as *Homo erectus* or even *Homo ergaster* – although this would have been a very, very simple form of communication.

- **Language developed** as a way of maintaining relationships within groups.

- **Language** is different from cries of alarm or mating calls. It involves a system for representing ideas and feelings.

- **Speech** requires a long pharynx – a tube in the neck that runs up from the vocal cords (contained in the larynx) to the mouth.

- **In other primates** the pharynx is too short to produce complex modifications of sound.

- *Homo ergaster* had a longer pharynx than earlier hominids, suggesting that it was able to produce some basic speech.

- *Homo heidelbergensis* had an even longer pharynx and would have been able to produce complex sounds. However, its speech would have differed from ours because of the different shape of its face.

- **Neanderthals** would also have been able to speak. The fossil remains of a Neanderthal hyoid bone, which supports the larynx, is almost identical to a modern human's.

- **Modern speech** only developed with the arrival of *Homo sapiens*.

- **Some experts** think that modern speech first took place 100,000 years ago – others think it did not happen until around 40,000 years ago.

▶ *The differences between a chimpanzee (top) and a modern human (bottom) mean that the human is capable of speech, but the chimpanzee is not. Unlike chimpanzees and early hominids, we have long throats and shorter muzzles. Therefore our pharynxes can produce a range of sounds and our tongues can move backwards and forwards in our mouths to utter these sounds.*

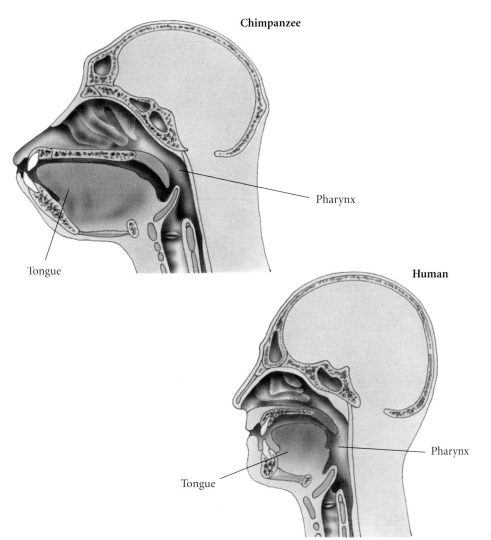

Chimpanzee

Pharynx

Tongue

Human

Pharynx

Tongue

Tools

▶ Homo habilis *produced flakes of stone, such as this one, by striking one stone against another, called a hammerstone.*

Stone tool

- **The greatest number** of *Homo habilis* tools has been found in the Olduvai Gorge in Tanzania. They include rocks that were used as hammers, flakers, choppers and scrapers.

- ***Homo habilis*** used these tools to cut meat and, especially, to scrape open animal bones to eat the marrow inside.

- **The stone tools** used by *Homo habilis* are crude and basic. This hominid was the first toolmaker, but, hardly surprisingly, it was not a skilled one.

- **But making** these early stone tools was still a challenging task – the toolmaker needed to strike one rock with another so that it would produce a single, sharp flake rather than shattering into many pieces.

- **Toolmaking requires** considerable intelligence. It involves the use of memory, as well as the ability to plan ahead and to solve abstract problems.

▶ Homo ergaster *used hammers made of bone to produce thinner and sharper flakes of stone.*

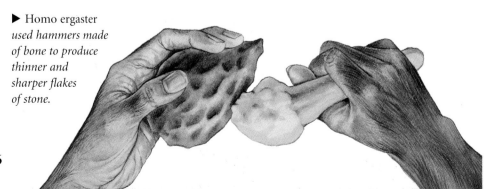

▼ Early humans developed more and more sophisticated methods of killing animals, including weapons, traps and fire.

Index